GOD
IS A VERY PRESENT HELP

BARBARA NELSON

WESTBOW
PRESS
A DIVISION OF THOMAS NELSON

WestBow Press books may be ordered through
booksellers or by contacting:

WestBow Press
A Division of Thomas Nelson
1663 Liberty Drive
Bloomington, IN 47403
www.westbowpress.com
1-(866) 928-1240

ISBN: 978-1-4497-9694-5 (sc)
ISBN: 978-1-4497-9693-8 (e)

Library of Congress Control Number: 2013909914

Printed in the United States of America.

WestBow Press rev. date: 06/05/2013

This book is dedicated to: JjW, Bridgette-Ruth, June W, Hyacinth, Audré, Deon, Carol, the two sisters, to "332".

And

To the Memory of my parents
Fred & Lucille Jones

Table of Contents

Preface

Many people, during the course of their lives go through a difficult emotional experience. The event could change them—either for better or for worse—for the remainder of their lives.

Some people carry the negative experience for a long time and constantly refer to the event wherever they are. Others learn from the difficulty, rise to a new level of consciousness, and move on to a new and more fulfilling life.

The Holy Bible is filled with promises of God's help in time of trouble and of His assurance that we can overcome any stumbling block we may encounter in our life's path.

In "**God is a Present Help**" the author tells of her experience in searching for God's answer to a very distressing and negative life experience and of her delight in finding the right promise that brought her out of the pit of despair into a new and promising existence.

Introduction:
Divine Appointments and
Divine Connections

God is. I know that.

The Holy Bible says He is our Refuge.

He is our Strength.

He is A Very Present Help in time of trouble.

The renowned English poet Alfred Lord Tennyson in **"The Higher Pantheism" 1869** says, "Speak to Him thou for He hears, and Spirit with Spirit can meet—Closer is He than breathing, and nearer than hands and feet."[1]

God permits certain unpleasant, disturbing and difficult situations to take place in our lives. I do not know why, but the Bible does say in 1 Peter 5: 10 ". . . **after that ye have suffered a while . . ."**[2]. That refers to you and me.

Some Christian preachers say that God not only permits, but also ordains certain difficult and hard situations to occur in our lives.

We read in the Bible in 1 Peter 4:12 **"Beloved, think it not strange concerning the fiery trial which is to try you, as though some strange thing happened unto you . . ."**[3]

For most of my life I thought that verse applied only to great, powerful, well-known, Christian folk. The ones we read about in books and magazines, and hear their amazing stories told on radio and television.

Surely that Bible verse could not include a simple, ordinary, humble, unknown believer like me.

I had to change my mind!

Why? You may ask . . .

I went through **a fiery trial.**

"The "fiery trial," then is not a strange thing which happens only to a few of the Lord's family, but is more or less the appointed lot of all," says J.C. Philpott, the eminent English Christian writer (1802-1869). This quotation is taken from an article by Philpott published in **'Daily Portions'** online January 13, 2013.[4]

But God's promise in Zechariah 13:9 is ***"I will bring the third part through the fire and will refine them as silver is refined, and will try them as gold is tried: they shall call on my name and I will hear them . . ."*** [5]

∽ ● ∽

Many Christian people believe that our lives are "pruned" during the times of difficulty. This, they say, enables us "to bear more and better fruit."

What I have come to realize is that if we do not believe in God, if we do not know at least some of His promises, if we cannot or do not trust Him we will fail hopelessly in the times of difficulty. We will easily succumb to the stress and collapse under the pressure of a difficult, fiery, situation.

But if, on the other hand, we have the tenacity to hold on to the tiny light of our faith in God, we will eventually ***"after that ye have suffered a while"*** [6] come out on the other side of the trial.

We will come out as much stronger, wiser persons because of the experience. Then each one of us can say, ***"It is good for me that I have been afflicted, that I might learn thy statutes."*** [7]

It is my firm belief that God, in His omniscience, His mercy and His love sets up Divine Appointments and Divine Connections to aid every single person who will go through a life crisis, or a deeply troubling situation.

If we believe in God, if we acknowledge His Presence and Power, if we have faith, as tiny as **"*a grain of mustard seed*",**[8] if we know how to listen for **"*the still, small voice*",**[9] we will overcome or come through the trial.

We come through the thick, murky darkness and the pain of the trial because of our faith in God **and** with the assistance of the Divine Appointments and Divine Connections set up by Almighty God himself.

∽ ● ∽

Some Ministers of the Gospel and Bible scholars affirm that the story recorded in St. John's Gospel, Chapter 4 where Jesus meets with the woman of Samaria at Jacob's well in the city of Sychar is an example of a Divine Appointment.

But just what is a Divine Appointment? Do Divine Appointments really take place? Are there Divine Connections?

In my humble opinion **Divine Appointments** do take place. I believe that A Divine Appointment is a meeting between people that is arranged by Almighty God Himself, a meeting that will greatly assist one or both persons. The appointment will change, enhance, deliver and possibly even save the life of one (or both) of the persons involved.

I also believe that God sets up **Divine Connections**. What may appear to the casual onlooker or even to the people involved, as a chance meeting with another human being may very well be a Divine Connection. That connection will dramatically alter, help, assist or preserve one's life. In fact, without the Divine Connection a person could possibly lose his/her life.

Maybe these are imperfect explanations. However, I can only speak from my own personal experience. In hindsight I know absolutely and I have experienced totally that God, the all-knowing, all seeing One does save, help, protect and deliver. Very often He does a great and mighty work through what we may consider a chance meeting.

The Great God, Creator and Sustainer of the Universe, is the One who says . . . "*I am the Lord, and there is none else, there is no God beside me.*"[10] "*I am God, and there is none like me. Declaring the end from the beginning, and from ancient times the things that are not yet done.*"[11]

I write this story in thanksgiving and praise to God the Almighty, to God Most High. It is my sincere hope and prayer that some person who is even now in deep despair and emotional suffering, someone who is very depressed and reads this true story will find new hope; that he or she will believe that God can be trusted in **all** things; that someone who is in the deep, dark pit of despondency, who can see no way out of a crisis; *who is perhaps even at this very moment on the brink of suicide* will take courage and hold on to the thought that God will come through, God will deliver. God will work through a human agent, a divine connection.

I have come to realize that many people, at some time or other in their lives, experience a devastating event—a very unpleasant, unwholesome, traumatic, unexpected and emotionally destructive situation. More often than not the event sneaks in unheralded and unexpected. A person who is a confidante, a "friend"—a "*trusted* friend" or even a close relative, may in fact, orchestrate the event.

The experience could leave one permanently bitter, totally frustrated, emotionally crippled, absolutely humiliated and unhinged. There could be the temptation to lash out at the injustice, to perhaps, take legal action and fight (on the human level) for what he or she considers to be one's rights.

But, dear one, if you are even now going through a very traumatic experience, look for God's deliverance in the midst of the fire, as the three

Hebrew boys, Shadrach, Meshach and Abed-nego did.[12]. Believe with all your heart that *the fourth man* will appear.

Remember God's promises **"never to leave you or forsake you,"**[13] to be with you **"when you pass through the waters**".[14] He has promised in the book of Isaiah: **"When you go through deep waters, I will be with you. When you go through rivers of difficulty, you will not drown. When you walk through the fire of oppression, you will not be burned up; the flames will not consume you.**"[15]

Trust Him! Please trust Him. **He cannot fail and He will not fail you**. He promised in Isaiah: **"I will lead them in paths that they have not known. I will make darkness light before them and crooked things straight. These things will I do unto them and not forsake them."**[16] That means you and me! God will not forsake you! Put all your trust absolutely in God.

When the deep darkness and the pain seem to be unbearable then cry out! Cry out to God as David did in Psalm 6: **"Have mercy upon me, O Lord, for I am weak . . . My soul is also sore vexed . . . deliver my soul; Oh save me for thy mercies sake."**[17]

We must believe that God knows everything. We must accept that He is our Heavenly Father—a loving and compassionate father. If we do accept this and if we cling to His promises then we will survive the devastation and the awful feelings of abject loneliness, shame, sorrow and severe anxiety that often accompany the unwelcome situation.

If we truly believe and ". . . . **know that in all things God works for the good of those who love him, who have been called according to his purpose,"**[18] then we will survive. We will survive because if God is for us then **no one** can overcome us. We will live through the hard times, the unexpected, harsh, bitter and alien experiences, the shame or the betrayal. **We will overcome the temptation to end our earthly life**.

A new dawn will break—a dawn that we can greet with joy and happy anticipation rather than with anxiety, tears and despair.

As time passes we will find new strength, both physical and spiritual strength, we will accomplish new things, have new and amazing experiences and we will discover new friends and companions. We will live life on a higher Plane while our faith in God will grow deeper and stronger. We will have greater trust in God and greater commitment to serve Him, know Him and obey Him.

It will not happen overnight, no not by any means.

We have to wait on God's timing and His timing is definitely not like our own.

In Psalm 27 David says, **"Wait on the Lord, be of good courage and He shall strengthen thine heart: wait, I say, on the Lord."**[19]

Again, he says in Psalm 37: **". . . wait patiently for Him."**[20]

And in the same Psalm, verse 34: **"Wait on the Lord and keep his way."**[21]

In Psalm 130 the writer says: **"I wait for the Lord, my soul doth wait, and in his word do I hope."**[22]

Waiting is the most difficult thing to do when you are out of a job, without shelter, without money, without family, dependent on charity or the kindness of strangers in order to live from one day to the next.

But there is no other way! We have to wait on God.

If we try to get out of our difficulty on only our own steam or by manipulating a situation we are going to fail. We will be like a person thrashing around in quicksand, the more we struggle the deeper we will get in the mire.

That does not mean that we give up trying to find a solution. What it does mean is that we try and then wait to see if God's Presence is involved in the process. When we get a clear answer, when the light breaks through the darkness and His peace comes over us, then we know we are on our way out of the difficulty. Psalm 85: 8 (KJV) says: ***"I will hear what God the Lord will speak: for he will speak peace unto his people, and to his saints; but let them not turn again to folly."***[23]

The problem has been solved.

The process may take a long time—it usually takes much, much longer than we would want, but the dawn of a better day will break and the end of the trauma will come.

Believe me.

Why?

I know. I have experienced it.

"Hannah"

I had spent some time in the United States and on my return home I decided to stay at a modest guesthouse for a few days prior to moving into a new apartment.

It was wonderful for me to be at home. The familiar sights and sounds of the island refreshed my spirit. I slept soundly on the first night I returned home.

Breakfast the following morning was very welcome. The meal was delicious.

A tall. slender, dark-skinned young woman served at my table. She said very little. Her manner was quiet and reserved and she smiled shyly when I greeted her. She hovered about my table, quickly filling my cup with fresh coffee and bringing more toast when I had eaten what was on my plate.

She had a gentle, peaceful spirit. As I watched her perform her duties with avidity in the dining room I felt a prompting inside me to find out more about her. I felt that maybe I ought to help her.

In the months that followed I realized that feeling was the prompting of the Holy Spirit.

When I got up to leave the table I left a generous tip for her under my breakfast plate. I walked out of the dining hall, turned the corner and went up the stairs that lead to my room. As I was half the way up the stairs, I heard a voice calling out: "Miss! Miss!"

I looked back and saw the young woman who had served at my table walking quickly toward me.

"Yes, my dear," I said, as I looked down at her standing at the foot of the stairs. "Is something the matter?"

"Yes, Miss, you left this on the table!" she said holding out the money to me.

I walked quickly down the stairs and said quietly to her: "That is for you!"

"Oh! Thank you! Thank you very much!" she said and smiled shyly.

"You are welcome," I answered. "What is your name?"

"My name is Hannah," she said.

"I am happy to know you Hannah," I replied.

Little did I know that the meeting I had with Hannah that morning was a **Divine Connection**.

2

A wonderful opportunity is born

Bear ye one another's burdens, and so fulfill the law of Christ.

—Galatians 6 v: 2

For the remainder of the time that I spent at the guesthouse I got to know Hannah better. She was an orphan. Her parents had died when she was a youngster. She was not highly educated, but she was very ambitious and determined to improve herself.

She was in her early thirties and lived in the inner city; she was a single mother of two boys. The older boy was about to leave secondary school while the younger was just about to leave junior school and enter secondary school.

Hannah demonstrated a quiet determination in everything that she did and she was passionate about having her rights.

As I listened to her on the few occasions that we spoke I was impressed with her integrity, her calmness and her good work ethic. An idea was forming in my mind. I would try to help this young woman financially.

I did not say anything to her about the idea that I had. When I left the guesthouse I gave her a gift of money and promised that I would keep in touch with her.

From that time onward I did all that I could to assist Hannah. Soon I migrated to the United States and I continued to help her. Her appreciation was always heartwarming.

We kept in touch. We corresponded by mail and ever so often I would 'phone her. She continued to work at the guesthouse and took advantage of any training courses that were offered there.

For my own part my life had moved in what I considered to be a very positive and secure direction. Things were evolving quietly and smoothly. I felt very much at peace about my future.

Towards the end of 2010 a wonderful opportunity began to take shape on the horizon of my professional life. I was invited to work on a dream project. This was something that would not only challenge and satisfy me intellectually but also fill the financial void left in my life by the lack of a pension. I felt secure, happy and assured for perhaps the first time in many, many years.

"Everything Crash!"

"Now the serpent was more subtle than any beast of the field which the Lord God had made. And he said unto the woman, Yea, hath God said, Ye shall not eat of every tree of the garden?" Genesis 3 v 1 [1]

Just as the wheels of the **"wonderful opportunity"** started moving, however, the proverbial train skidded and derailed!

"Everything crash!"[2] That was the title of the first big hit done by a well-known Jamaican rock steady vocal group known as "The Ethiopians", in 1968.

"Everything crash!" That was how my life appeared as the year 2010 gave way to 2011.

Why?

The serpent entered the Garden of Eden.

The bubble of opportunity burst. By itself? No! Not at all.

Ephesians 6:12 says: **"For we wrestle not against flesh and blood, *but against principalities, against powers, against the rulers of the darkness of this world, against spiritual wickedness in high places."*[3]**

I was lured into a well-prepared trap and while my guard was down I foolishly swallowed the bait. Suddenly my usually well-ordered, peaceful and quiet life was thrown into disorder, disarray and confusion.

I was never more terrified in my entire life.

I remembered a verse in Job: **"The snare is laid for him in the ground and a trap for him in the way."[4]**

Because of certain things I said in my frustration, anxiety and bitterness everything that I cherished and valued in my life at that time figuratively exploded and disintegrated.

I found myself at the worst place that I had ever been in my entire life—and believe me I had been in some tough places before.

I was ostracized. I was mocked. I was treated like a leper. There was nowhere for me to turn; there was no one to turn to. I was figuratively and almost literally put out on the street. ". . . *fear was on every side while they took counsel together against me . . .*"[5]

The punishment for my "sin" did not fit the crime!

Dear God Almighty, I cried out in my anguish, why? Why? Why?

In Psalms 55:12 David cries out: ". . . *it was not an enemy that reproached me; then I could have borne it: neither was it he that hated me that did magnify himself against me; then I would have hid myself from him . . .*"[6]

I could identify with David and I fully understood what he said to Gad the prophet, *"I am in a great strait: let us fall into the hand of the Lord for his mercies are great and let me not fall into the hands of man."*[7]

Some laughed at my calamity, some snickered, some felt justified at my hurt, some were very happy to watch me fall.

But God . . .

God, the all-powerful, great and awesome God, is merciful. He knows that many of us are fragile creatures: *"**For he knoweth our frame he remembereth that we are dust.**"*[8] We are prone to sin and mistakes, and yet, He still loves us. He loves us with an everlasting love.

He forgives, He binds up our wounds, He runs to meet us when, like the prodigal son, we *"**arise and go**"*[9] to Him.

Not so some proud self-righteous human beings who stand aloof, smirk and gloat with joy when another human falters and makes a mistake. How puffed up and indignant they become, while they behold the mote in the eye of the offender and forget the beam in their own eye![10]

Many months later I realized that there is yet another angle from which to view the times of difficulty and pain that often challenge God's people. I learned this when I read a column, published online **(October 7, 2012),** from the writings of J. C. Philpot[11]. In one of the **Daily Portions** he writes:

> *"We often find that those very times when God's people think they are faring ill, are the seasons when they are really faring well; and again, at other times, when they think they are faring well, then they are really faring ill.*
>
> *For instance, when their souls are bowed down with trouble, it often seems to them that they are faring ill. God's hand appears to be gone*

out against them: he has hidden his face from them; they can find no access to a throne of grace; they have no sweet testimonies from the Lord that the path in which he is leading them is one of his choosing, and that all things will end well with them. This they think is indeed faring ill, and yet perhaps they never fare better than when under these circumstances of trouble, sorrow, and affliction. These things wean them from the world.

"If they were setting up, and bowing down to idols in the chambers of imagery, affliction and trouble smite them to pieces before their eyes, take away their gods, and leave them no refuge but the Lord God of hosts."

That was where I found myself. I had indeed been bowing down to an idol.

How very true.

But now my soul was bowed down with trouble. There seemed no way out; all I could think of was finding an end to the searing emotional pain, the deep soul sorrow, and the constant darkness that enveloped my mind.

Day after day I could see no light, no apparent way out. As David cried out when he fled from Absalom his son. I too cried out to Almighty God: *"Lord, how are they increased that trouble me! . . .*

Many there be which say of my soul, there is no help for him in God."[12]

The great darkness continued week after week, month after month. My faith wavered and wilted. My body grew tired and thin. I was in unfamiliar territory where despair, doubt and despondency became my constant and only companions.

I felt like the writer of Psalm 102 who said in verse 4: *"My heart is smitten and withered like grass, so that I forget to eat my bread."*[13]

Winter came and went.

My attempt at rapprochement was summarily rebuffed.

As spring gave way to summer and summer made way for autumn I continued to apply for employment. I went to several interviews. Not even one worked out.

What was I to do?

Oh my God! Was there no hope for me?

A big disappointment!

"So do not throw away your confidence; it will be richly rewarded. You need to persevere so that when you have done the will of God, you will receive what He has promised."

—**Hebrews 10: 35-36 NIV¹**

Then, suddenly, after many, many months of disappointment, fear and frustration, I was promised employment. It felt like the sun breaking through storm clouds! The offer came through the help of a friend.

It was wonderful! Just wonderful!

At last something was moving for me. I was quietly hopeful and expectant.

For over a week almost every day I had several long telephone conversations with my prospective employer. I sent her my Resume. She said she liked what she saw. Everything appeared to be settled. I was looking forward to employment . . . at last.

"You are overqualified for this job, but please do not disappoint me and take another job," my 'future' employer urged me. "I really want you to come to me!"

I assured her I would go to no one else and would wait for her. And I honestly meant what I said even though I had received an email from another person at a well-known institution.

She lived some distance away from where I was staying. One week later she met with me late one Saturday evening. We sat in her car with her husband and children and had a pleasant time getting to know each other.

Everything seemed to be perfect . . . except for one thing. Her husband sat slumped down by the steering wheel of the car, his dark face hidden in shadow. He said very little—if anything. His silence was so pronounced and I found it so peculiar that I asked the woman, "Is your husband always so quiet?"

"Hahaha" she laughed shrilly (and rather nervously I thought) then said, "Yes, he is a very quiet person!"

I felt that his silence was rather ominous, after all this was an interview! But as I embraced the arrival of employment I brushed aside the niggling feeling of anxiety that gnawed like a hungry rodent at the edge of my mind.

The woman and I agreed on a time that she (and her family) would come for me the next morning—a Sunday. I went to bed with a smile on my face and gratitude in my heart. At long last I would be employed.

I awoke early, got dressed and was ready to go.

My friend, Joan, helped me to get my two suitcases downstairs and placed at the front door. I was due to leave in an hour.

"Are you happy to go, Barbara?" Joan asked me, a little wistfully, I thought.

"I am happy and sad," I said after a while. "I'm happy to be getting employment. A little sad to leave the place that has become my home."

Then my cell phone rang.

I did not recognize the number.

"Hello," I said into the phone.

"Barbara?" a female voice said.

I recognized the person's voice.

The woman with whom I had spoken several times, who had asked me not to take any other job and who had met with me the previous Saturday evening called to tell me that her husband had changed his mind. They no longer needed me.

"We fussed about the situation all night!" she said in a tight high-pitched voice. "I really want you to come but I have to go along with what he says," she said.

Really?

Really!

To say I was very disappointed is putting it mildly. I think I was more shocked and dismayed than disappointed!

Yet, on the heels of the feeling of disappointment I knew in my spirit that God had a hand in the matter. **HE DID NOT WANT ME TO GO TO THAT FAMILY.**

Why?

I do not know.

But that is what I felt.

I was disappointed, but, to my surprise, I was not overwhelmed and in despair.

Joan, who had given me shelter for several months, felt the same way.

"Do not fret!" she cautioned me in a stern voice, "as long as I am here I will help you. You will not go hungry. There is a reason why God prevented you going even though it was at the last minute! Maybe He saved you from an accident on the road. Whatever it is, God knows!"

What came to my mind in the midst of the disappointment was the story of Abraham and his son. God Almighty waited until the patriarch was about to plunge the knife into his son's heart before his angel prevented him from doing so.

God's timing is His own business!

Who am I to question God's timing? Who am I to try and understand His ways? All I am expected to do is to trust Him—in all things!!

It was a hard blow, a bitter pill to swallow, but I consoled myself that I had taken a big step. I had *almost* found good employment.

Another story came to my mind that morning. It was the story told In 1 Samuel 30 of what happened when David and his men returned to Ziglag. They found out that the enemy had destroyed the place and taken their wives and children captive. It was a most distressing situation. The people spoke of stoning David . . . **"*but David encouraged himself in the Lord his God.*"[2]**

I was pleased with myself that after waiting for so long I did not break down at that moment, neither did I become hysterical or flounder helplessly in despair. I really tried to encourage myself. I felt that if I had come so close to finding employment surely something would turn up! I would keep on trying.

Sometime later, after the days, weeks and months that I went through the life crisis I came across an inspiring article written by **Jeff Doles** (with his wife, the founders of Walking Barefoot Ministries). The title of the piece was **"How to encourage yourself in the Lord."[3]**

The writer says **"discouragement is an indication that you are walking by sight, not by faith."** He suggests that when discouragement comes and we find that we have been walking by sight instead of by faith, it is time to go back to the scriptures and let the promises of God build our faith back up to strength.

Still no answer . . .

"No weapon that is formed against thee shall prosper; and every tongue that shall rise against thee in judgment thou shalt condemn."

—*Isaiah 54 v: 17 (KJV)* [1]

In an effort to relieve the anxiety, the boredom and emotional listlessness (and also with the hope of finding employment) I had volunteered at a Retirement Home many miles away. I served there for several months and thoroughly enjoyed what I had to do. I met many new and interesting people and, in addition, I learned new skills.

But as the days turned into weeks and the weeks became months, I realized that the paltry sum of money I had was just about gone—used up in train and bus fares.

Ever so often the waves of hopelessness and fear threatened to engulf me. Depression washed over my soul. I felt that there was very little hope for me; I could see no light at the end of the proverbial tunnel. I did not see a way out. Here I was among strangers, without hope, without a job. I often felt very depressed and sorry for myself.

On more than one occasion I almost gave up trying to find employment.

One Friday night I became so depressed and despondent that I seriously considered not how but where to end my life.

Daily I cried out in my spirit, *"Father God where are you? Do you hear me crying out to you? Why is there no answer from you Lord?"*

The tide begins to turn

"Therefore take no thought, saying, what shall we eat? or, What shall we drink? Or, Wherewithal shall we be clothed?"

—*St. Matthew 6 v. 31*[1]

Many, many more weeks would pass by during which time I struggled to overcome the anxiety, the frustration, the fear, doubt and despair . . . then, some unusual, and wonderful things began to happen in my life.

Money started to trickle in to me from the most unexpected sources!

"If it had not been the Lord who was on our side, now may Israel say; If it had not been the Lord who was on our side, when men rose up against us; Then they had swallowed us up

quick, when their wrath was kindled against us;" Psalm 124 (KJV)[2]

The amazing little changes in my life began without fanfare.

One evening after I had done a day's volunteering at the Retirement Home, I came off the train and stood awaiting the bus to reach the place where I stayed. A neatly attired young boy who carried a bag of what appeared to be schoolbooks came up to me. As he looked into my face he quietly but confidently asked me for two dollars to get home.

I looked in my change purse and there was a single five-dollar bill. *It was all the money I had to my name.*

I have always tried to give to anyone who asks of me. In **Matthew 5:42 Jesus says: "Give to him that asketh thee, and from him that would borrow of thee turn not thou away."[3]** It is not for me to judge whether or not it is a genuine need. So I gave the boy what was at that moment my last piece of money.

More tired and hungry after the long day than despondent over my situation I reached to the place where I stayed. I quietly went to my room.

Without bothering to turn on the light in the room, I used the light in the passageway. As I placed my bag on the couch I noticed something that appeared to be a piece of paper on the couch.

I picked up what I thought was a piece of paper to place in the trash basket.

But it was not a piece of paper.

It was a $20 bill.

Really?

Really!

In a few minutes I found out that Joan, the person who had given me shelter, had left it there,

"Why so?"

"I just had a feeling that you needed some money," she said.

Indeed!

Indeed!!

And so the trickle of financial supply and help began.

It came from Joan; it came from a young relative in Miami who worried that I was unable to make an appointment to see a doctor about the hypertension. A gift of money came to me from a close friend who was even then caring for her terminally ill husband. An out-of-work Christian schoolteacher, who I have never met, sent $30 "**just to help**" when she heard of my situation from an acquaintance, another friend in my island (we went to high school together) generously sent me some dollars; and two sisters ever so often sent $40 or $50 to help me.

This was the proverbial manna in the wilderness and I tithed every single financial gift that I received.

Then there was Althea who did not know me. She lived some distance away from me, but on hearing of my situation, quickly purchased some warm clothing and food and brought them to me just as the chilly October winds began to blow.

But it was not only the wonderful material gifts of shelter, money and clothing that touched my heart. There was also the tremendous emotional support I received from all these friends and also from faithful Carol, a quiet, reserved person, a generous caring soul and a great encourager.

Carol called me regularly. She ended every single conversation she had on the phone with me with the phrase: "Keep your hopes up! Something will come along."

Sometimes I wondered how she could possibly maintain such a cheerful and positive attitude when it appeared to me that my world had fallen apart and that I would never ever find employment again.

Carol would wait patiently for a call from me whenever she knew I had gone for an interview. There were many nights when, after I had travelled to some faraway place for an interview, I waited, cold and shivering at the bus stop for the last bus to reach "home".

Carol would become very anxious if I did not call to let her know that I had reached home safely. So I made an effort to always let her know when I had reached home.

Hannah

Honor and shame from no condition rise. Act well your part: there all the honor lies.
—Alexander Pope.[1]

Perhaps what amazed me most, however, was what happened with Hannah, the humble young woman who lived in the inner city far away on my Caribbean island.

Remember she had very meager resources. She had two children to care for and no husband.

I had called to tell her that I was in a bad place. No longer in my apartment, without a job or any means of support. I was therefore unable to send any money on a regular basis to help her.

The reality was that I had no idea when I would ever be able to send money to her again.

She knew how difficult it was for me to call her on the 'phone (I could no longer afford to buy phone cards) so she tried to call me as often as she could.

Several months after I told her of my dire situation she called me early one Saturday morning. Very quickly she told me to "collect something" at Western Union.

Me? Collect 'something' at Western Union?

"What do you mean Hannah?"

"Well, do you remember you sent me one hundred US dollars last year? I had put it away. I believe you need it now so I am sending it for you. Please take it and use it to help yourself," she said quickly before I could say a word.

Three months later, she did the same thing.

Many months later I heard from a source that she collected the tips she received on the job and put it all together to make up US$100 to send for me. And each time she did so, she spoke to me with great joy and encouragement.

She would call me on the phone to tell me that her prayer group at her church was praying for me. She encouraged and strengthened me.

On three occasions during the fourteen months that I languished *"in the wilderness"* without employment, without any visible means of support, this young woman stood by me giving me not only emotional support but also making her own great financial sacrifice to help me through what was arguably the most traumatic period of my entire life.

Without a doubt she was, and still is to this day a *Divine Connection* in my life.

8

A faithful friend

"He that is thy friend indeed,
He will help thee in thy need:
If thou sorrow, he will weep;
If thou wake, he cannot sleep:
Thus of every grief in heart
He with thee does bear a part.
These are certain signs to know
Faithful friend from flattering foe."[1]

—William Shakespeare

It must have been in the year 2007 when Deanne and I began to speak with each other on the phone. She was from the same Caribbean island as I was. We had spoken briefly from time to time while she was Editor of the newspaper that I wrote for. Then we started talking about 'stuff'—world news, the assassination of Benazir Bhutto, the Al Jazeera TV station, happenings back home, and the upcoming elections in the United States.

We talked a lot about a lot of things but what I liked about her was that she never gossiped. She did not mess around in other people's business.

Gradually it became a bit of a ritual—our long chats on a Saturday morning while her pot of soup was on the stove in her apartment, and my Crockpot was simmering with stewed chicken and vegetables in my kitchen.

I knew very little about her at first and she also knew very little about me. She lived near New York while I lived in Maryland. We were just two women who shared our ideas and opinions on a number of issues. Over time our relationship developed into a solid friendship.

The time came when I could share the good news with her that I was going to be part of a really exciting research project, the **dream project** I mentioned earlier. She was happy for me. She rejoiced with me, she was very thrilled at my good fortune.

Shortly after when the debacle took place, Deanne was perturbed and anxious about my well-being. She moved from being a telephone friend to my close confidante. Her courage, her devotion to our friendship, her words of advice and comfort helped me to go through the storm.

She was very upset at what had happened in my life and this deep concern for me propelled her into the top echelon of my small group of close friends.

Deanne was no fair-weather friend. It would have been so much easier for her and quite understandable if she had decided to back away from the ugly situation that had enveloped me.

She loyally stood by me through the many months of darkness and pain.

Sometimes when she telephoned me I was upbeat and cheerful—excited at the possibility of employment; at other times I was morbidly depressed or overcome with anxiety, but through it all she remained loyal to me.

Never a weekend passed without her calling to check on me, to offer hope, advice, support and encouragement. We often laughed when I reminded her that nether of us knew what the other one looked like. Yet we shared deep thoughts and ideas. Her spirituality, her strong faith, her honesty and goodness helped me to trust her and appreciate her more and more.

During this time I was pleased that I could offer her some comfort when her mother became ill and had to spend some time in hospital. We were both very grateful to God when her mother recovered her health.

Deanne became the wind beneath my wings. She gave me hope, encouragement and support while I went through the maelstrom. She stood with me during some of the darkest, dreariest and loneliest days of my entire life.

After many months had passed and I finally found suitable employment I emailed her to thank her in writing for the support and love she had shown to me during the dark, depressing days.

She replied so graciously and part of her email said:" *I called you as often as I did because I worried about you. I felt I needed to anchor you by reminding you, you were not alone.*

You are never far from my thoughts and you are always on my prayer list. God is walking with you. Be blessed, be loved, and take care."

Deanne is another **Divine Connection** in my life.

9

An unusual request

". . . Pray for one another . . ."

—*James 5 v: 16*[1]

A few years before the drama unfolded in my life another peculiar incident took place. The incident would greatly affect my destiny.

It was a few minutes before my lunch break at the office where I worked. I had been employed for just a few weeks and I was gradually getting to know the other people who worked there.

On the day in question I was standing quietly beside the photocopier sorting some files when I felt a hand on my shoulder. Before I could even turn around to see who it was, someone who was standing behind me spoke to me in a low female voice.

"Will you please pray for my mother?" the person said.

I turned around slowly and faced a slim, dark-skinned African-American woman. I recognized her as one of the people who worked in the office with me. She usually sat at the other end of the large L-shaped office.

"Y-y-yes, I will," I stammered. I was really quite surprised at the very unusual request.

This was a totally new experience for me—a stranger asking me to pray for her mother, someone that I did not even know!

Later that day as our paths crossed, I asked the woman why she had asked me, a stranger, to pray for her mother. After all, I said to myself, she did not know me well. She could not have known if I was an atheist or if I believed in God or even if I ever prayed!

She replied in a quiet but confident tone: "I see the Spirit of God on you."

I must admit I was once more very surprised, totally blown away at that remark. I was also more than a little apprehensive . . .

What if she had seen the spirit of evil on me, I thought to myself.

Over the following weeks we said hello when our paths crossed. Her name was Joan and I noticed that she was quiet, dignified and soft-spoken. She never took part in the gossip sessions that were a regular feature of the office milieu.

Whenever we met in the lobby, on the elevator, or in the lunchroom, I enquired about her mother's condition. She was always hopeful and positive. Some years later, however, she told me that she was grateful for something I said to her one day.

On that occasion I had asked how her mother was doing. Her response revealed that while she was deeply concerned at the changes in her mother's condition she still hoped for a turnaround in her health. Without thinking of her feelings I said to her, "It will only get worse. I know. My mother had Alzheimer's too."

Maybe it was brutal on my part to give her the raw truth, but some years later she told me it was better for her to accept the truth at that time than to keep on hoping for something that would never happen.

I left that position some months later. Although we were not great friends at the time, Joan and I had a very cordial relationship and we respected each other. We kept in touch with the occasional telephone call, but as time went on we spoke only occasionally.

10

Joan

*"And now my soul is poured out upon me; the
days of affliction have taken hold upon me."*

—Job 30 v: 16[1]

Several months later as it slowly began to dawn
on me that something cold, dark, shadowy and
detrimental to my emotional, professional and
physical wellbeing was coming against me I
remembered Joan and decided to give her a
call.

It was by no means a call to her for help, per se.
Rather the thought *"just came to me"* to call her
and say hello.

When she answered the phone and I told her I
was calling her response was: "Is that really you,
Barbara?

I have been praying that I would hear from you. How are you?"

I did not tell her then that I was terrified, scared and extremely fearful about what I suspected was going on around me.

"Please keep in touch. Call me whenever you can and take care of yourself," she said when we ended the brief call.

That short call was a lifeline for me. At that point neither Joan nor I had the slightest idea of the devastation that would take place in my life. Neither of us could foresee the important role she would play in my survival.

Time would prove to us both that we had a **Divine Connection.**

Agape Love

"Yea, though I walk through the valley of the shadow . . ."

—*Psalm 23 v: 4.*[1]

Without going into all the details of the sordid, ugly and frightening experience, suffice it to say that I was destitute.

Joan opened her home to me. She gave me the keys to her house and shared whatever she had with me.

She was a quiet, peaceful person. She said all that mattered to her was that "her sister" needed help and she was prepared to give that help for as long as it took. I believed she meant every word that she said.

Why, I wondered, did this woman who was not my family, or close confidante at that time go out of her way to assist me? Why did she make so many sacrifices to help me? She explained to me one day that it was her understanding of agape love. It was her mantra.

Agape love is *"selfless, sacrificial and unconditional."*[2]

Several nights each week, I stayed by myself alone in her apartment while she stayed at her mother's apartment to take care of her.

I was bothered and greatly embarrassed that while I remained with her she had to spend extra money on utilities and groceries. She even offered to buy me some new clothes. But she never made me feel that I was a burden nor did she ever make mention of the extra expenses. She was gracious, caring and compassionate.

One of her favorite scriptures was from Psalm 23. She played a recording of the psalm every weekend before she left home for service at her church.

"Yea though I walk **through** the valley," she would say to me over and over again especially when my faith floundered and flickered.

"You are going **through**, Barbara," she would say confidently as she pointed her manicured finger at me. "You are going to come out of the valley of the shadow one day, my sister!"

Those were some of the times when I would break down and cry. I would cry because my faith had become so weak and because *"one day"* seemed as elusive as a will-o'-the-wisp.

I would cry because I could see no end to my emotional suffering and financial bankruptcy. I would cry because I was holding the anguish and bitterness of the negative experience so close to my heart and I would not, could not or did not want to let it go. I was in the **"valley of Achor"**[3] where worry, fear and confusion were my constant companions. I could not find the hope.

But while I was preoccupied with my own unhappy circumstance, I realized that Joan was going through her own emotional storm. Her beloved mother was getting weaker. On more than one occasion while she stayed with her, Joan had to call 911 and have her mother rushed to the hospital.

Those were the times when my heart went out to her as I saw the tiredness in her eyes and heard the anxiety in her voice. The situation drew me out of my own immediate concerns. It made me reflect on the legacy of my own parents who had passed on some years before. I gave thanks to God that I had the awesome privilege to be with each one of them until the very moment they passed on.

While I stayed at Joan's apartment I was honored to meet her mother—"Big Mamma" as she was affectionately called. She was a sweetheart, a simple, gentle, loving, and generous African-American woman. I could clearly understand Joan's devotion to her.

A couple months before "Big Mamma" passed, I took some dollars out of my meager supply and bought her a bunch of pink carnations. I will forever remember the warm hug and radiant smile she gave me.

"Are these for me?" she asked in her soft husky voice.

"Yes, all for you," I answered as I kissed her cheek.

"Oh! Thank you, Jesus!" she said, looked up to heavens and then gave me another hug.

Some weeks later "Big Mamma" was once again in the hospital. This time she stayed for a much longer period than before. I felt in my spirit that her time for transition had come. Joan kept on hoping against hope that her mother would come through the crisis again, she did not want to let her beloved mother leave her.

But "Big Mamma" passed on.

Joan was devastated. Her mother passed, not on, but the very day after her own birthday. I watched her closely as she grappled with her grief, and tried to give her all the support I could. Through it all she carried herself with great dignity and poise.

Bridgette-Ruth

"Entreat me not to leave thee, or to return from following after thee, for whither thou goest, I will go; and where thou lodgest, I will lodge . . ."
Ruth 1 v 6[1]

Love

Compassion

Devotion

Sacrifice

13

Wait

"All the days of my appointed time will I wait till my change come." Job 14:14[1]

Time passed . . . ever so slowly. A new year dawned and with it came renewed hope in my heart. My faith grew strong once again. Maybe now, with a new year, a breakthrough would come for me, I thought.

January came in with a flurry of activity. Within about ten days I had three interviews. One interview was with a man who lived quite a distance from me. I travelled by bus and metro to meet him on a cold, dark, rainy day. He asked me to sit in his car in the car park at the train station, while he explained what the job was all about. The place where he lived, he said, was several miles away, so we had the interview in his car.

He was very nebulous and ambiguous about just what he wanted. He was separated from his wife, he said, so he needed a personal assistant housekeeper companion to him and his teenage son . . . I came away feeling confused and more than a little apprehensive about the position. When he called me a few days later, I declined the offer.

In the same week of that interview I started some free-lance work as a researcher/writer for a contact that I found on the Internet. But that assignment fizzled out quickly when I saw the paltry payment I received for the many long hours of hard work and research.

There was also another interview with a man who required someone to live in and manage a house he planned to rent to two professional people.

Then in mid-January came the incident with the woman who turned me down at the last minute.

February came and went. Once again I felt that finding suitable employment seemed like a pipe dream. After all there were so many people, just like me, who could not find employment.

March rolled in.

But wait!

On the second day of March that year two incidents took place. First I applied for a job on the Internet that wanted *"hardworking, honest women over fifty years of age."*

I was thrilled to receive a prompt reply . . .

But I was less than thrilled when I learned that the position was for a "personal adult film". It would pay $2000 for two hours of "work"!

The second incident occurred later that same day. While I was reading some inspirational material I came across a verse of scripture that stayed with me. It was: **"All the days of my appointed time will I wait till my change come."²**

I spent many hours meditating on the words. What I gained from that verse centered around *"appointed time"*, *"wait"* and *"my change come"*.

The time was appointed.

Did God appoint it?

That's what the scripture indicated.

I had the distinct feeling then that I still had some more waiting to do. The change would come. *I could not on my own make the change, **it would***

come. In the meanwhile I would have to **go through** the situation.

∽●∽

When at last God opened the door to employment for me it was nearly fourteen months to the day after I came to stay with Joan.

She was very happy that a new opportunity had come for me and so gracious when I thanked her for all the sacrifices she had made to help me through my time of distress.

"This will always be your home!" she said to me just before I departed. "You come back here whenever you want to."

The many months of waiting and trying and hoping and then seeing only failure, disappointment and emptiness had been emotionally draining, mentally difficult and financially very embarrassing for me.

14

Forgive us as we forgive

"And when ye stand praying, forgive, if ye have aught against any: that your Father also which is in heaven may forgive you your trespasses."
Mark 11:25 KJV[1]

But I have gone ahead of myself! I have omitted a most important part of the story. It could, in fact, be the lynchpin of the drama that played out in my life at that time.

In the several months that I kept applying for jobs, needing to be meaningfully employed in order to support myself, I was burdened with a great heaviness—an emotional weight, inside me. It was almost a physical pain. I kept thinking over and over again: How could this situation have happened? Why did the people involved act in the way they did? Was there no love? Did they have hearts of stone? I carried the heavy emotional trauma close to my heart.

Although I kept repeating the words **"Fret not thyself,"**[2], I felt that it was impossible for me to ever forgive the acts of cruelty and the subterfuge. I just could not!

At that time I did not fully comprehend the meaning of the scripture: **"God will not let you be tempted (tested) beyond what you can bear,"**[3], I did not realize that with His power within me I could survive the trial; that I had in me the God-given ability to go through the test and come out successfully. I had not put into effect the directive in **"Cast your burden upon the Lord and He will sustain you."**[4]. I was holding on tightly to the burden and trying to carry it all by myself.

But as the days, weeks and months passed I made a more determined effort to go deeper into and understand and obey God's Word. As I read books and articles by enlightened teachers and listened to certain anointed speakers on Christian television I realized more than ever that God's Word is **"more to be desired than gold, yea, than much fine gold; sweeter also than honey and the honeycomb"**.[5]

Although I had always read my Bible and meditated on scripture, this was a time of 'graduate study', increased learning and reflection. I soon realized during this time that one of the things I had to do to get out of the quagmire was to cease 'beating up on myself', forgive myself for my mistake, forgive all the players involved and let the whole incident go.

I had no choice. There was no other way! The whole negative experience was like an albatross hanging around my neck.

Every door I had approached did not or could not open. I was stuck. My life was standing still. I was neither going forward nor going backward. Something had to give.

And so, difficult as it was for my bruised and battered ego, my loss of dignity and my wounded self-esteem I repented and honestly forgave myself for the mistakes I had made, I forgave the cruelty of the people involved and let go of the ugly, sick, unwholesome situation.

I can clearly recall the afternoon when, while listening to a certain dynamic speaker on Christian Television I was convinced that he was speaking truth. He was speaking about the power of forgiveness.

But how, I said to myself, do I go through the process?

How can I be sure that I have forgiven and been forgiven?

As if in answer to my question, the speaker said: **"We forgive by faith, not by feelings. True forgiveness keeps on forgiving."**

I decided then and there to be obedient to the Word and walk the path of forgiveness. I could not carry the burden for even one moment more. It was too heavy, it was too corrosive, and it was crushing and destroying me.

For a few moments I could not believe I really had decided to let the whole awful burden go.

But I had to.

And I knew that I had!

I was so deeply convinced that this was what I had done that I immediately sent e-mail to the speaker on the program. I said in part **"For the past year I have been unable to move forward with my life because I have been stuck in unforgiveness. The situation is very painful . . ."**

A reply came back to me quickly. It said in part:

> **"We pray that, as you put real forgiveness into practice, that God will bless you with His peace and that you are comforted beyond measure**

knowing you are doing the perfect will of God. By your act you are now in a position to receive more blessings than you could ever believe, simply because you chose to do His will and serve Jesus. Be blessed!"

Many months later I came across this profound quote from Steve Maraboli. He writes in his book **Life, the Truth and Being Free:** *"The truth is, unless you let go, unless you forgive yourself, unless you forgive the situation, unless you realize that the situation is over, you cannot move forward."*[6]

The following day, after I had written to the speaker on Television and knew in my heart that I was now walking a new path, I told Joan that I had forgiven myself for the mistakes I had made and forgiven all the people who were the leading actors in the ongoing drama.

She listened calmly and quietly as I explained to her that I was now prepared to go forward with my life, on my own, alone, without any of their involvement or support. From that time onward I would rely only on the help and direction of Almighty God and the people that He would send into my life.

"God bless you, my sister," she replied quietly.

The wonderful thing I learned about the process of forgiveness is that we do not necessarily have to renew a relationship. We do not even have to speak to the person or persons involved, unless we really want to. It just means that we let the whole incident go. We no longer think about it or speak about it and allow it to disturb our minds and negatively affect our emotions and actions.

Thoughts of the incident or the people involved will try to creep back into our minds but we have the ability to brush the thoughts aside and ignore them. Shake them off! We need not dwell on the ugliness and the bitterness.

We can make a determined effort to replace those disturbing, haunting thoughts with other pleasant and uplifting thoughts or affirmations. After sometime the thoughts of the incident or the persons involved will come to mind less frequently until one day, wow, we realize that maybe a whole day has passed and the thoughts of the incident have not entered our minds—or rather we have not allowed the thoughts of the incident to enter our minds.

And then, wonder of wonders—whereas the incident was once uppermost in our mind clouding every waking moment and influencing every decision, now days will pass and not a thought about the incident or the people involved have come to mind. We feel lighter in our mind. We pray more effectively. We think more clearly. Then new doors begin to open. We are on our way out of the thick darkness.

In the absorbing Unity book **"The Lazarus Blueprint"** written by Mary-Alice and Richard Jafolla,[7] the authors compare the stone at the tomb of Lazarus (in the story recorded in the Bible in St. John Chapter 11) to something that is a block on your life's path. They say nothing can happen until you move the huge obstruction out of the way. The only way out is to forgive.

Maybe that was what happened in my own life, or maybe it was God's divine perfect timing.

What I do know is that after I decided to forgive and forget the cruel, demoralizing and heartbreaking incident, I started to feel lighter in my spirit. Gradually I felt my self-confidence and my feelings of self-worth return.

It took time—not as long as I expected it to take—but as I kept on working with the idea, I felt much better. I removed the stone of unforgiveness and loosed and let go the dead, decomposing corpse of what was once a beautiful, loving relationship.

I had started out on this unexpected and unwelcome journey as a weak, broken, demoralized and despondent creature. I was rather like a shattered clay vessel. I had been made to feel that I was a worthless human being, a failure, and a burden, someone without a future.

But I came out of the sordid mess stronger than I have ever been in my entire life. I was no longer a victim. I was an over comer.

I felt like tempered steel.

Eckhart Tolle writes in his Bestselling book, **"A New Earth, Awakening to Your Life's Purpose"**[8] that *"Life will give you whatever experience is most helpful for the evolution of your consciousness."*

I can relate strongly to what he says.

Some months later as I related the experience to Norma, one of my close friends, she reminded me of a quotation that we learned many years ago when we were teenage girls in high school. It is from a poem by Alfred Lord Tennyson and says: **"Men may rise on stepping stones of their dead selves to greater things."**[9]

I thank God for the experience—demoralizing, painful, bitter and debilitating as it was. If I had not gone through it I would never have known the amazing grace of God, the depth of His love and His awesome ability to rescue and save those who sincerely turn to Him in their time of trouble. I would not have experienced at first hand the true power of forgiveness.

Now I can say confidently and truthfully: *"The Lord is my helper, and I will not fear what man shall do unto me."*[10]

Now I appreciate more than ever the words: **"When the LORD turned again the captivity of Zion, *we were like them that dream. Then was our mouth filled with laughter, and our tongue with singing: then said they among the heathen, The Lord hath done great things for them."*[11]**

Now I know the reality of the words: *"And the Lord, He it is that doth go before thee: He will be with thee, He will not fail thee, neither forsake thee: fear not, neither be dismayed."*[12]

15

A new door opens

God knows the end from the beginning . . .[1]

∽ ● ∽

"All things work together for good to them that love God, to them who are the called according to his purpose." Romans 8: 28 KJV[2]

Exactly one week before my forgiveness experience, I had applied for yet another position. It was advertised on the Internet.

Things got off to a good start. It was a Thursday afternoon. After a pleasant telephone conversation with the agent an appointment was quickly set up for me to meet with the people on the following Saturday at noon.

On Saturday, however, just as I was about to leave the house to get to the train to travel (quite a distance) to meet with the people for the interview, I had a feeling—a prompting—that I should check my email—although I had checked it earlier that morning.

I could hardly believe my eyes when I saw an email that had been sent to me from the agent just a few moments before.

The meeting was postponed, he said, and apologized for the situation.

"Oh well! Here we go again! Déjà vu!" I said to myself . . . "another disappointment."

As I changed my clothes I decided to forget about that position and keep seeking for something else.

One week later, however, on the same day—a Thursday—just before I listened to the message on forgiveness, I got a feeling to check on the position. This was something that I had never done before—checking on a position after the interview had been postponed.

The agent told me the position was still not filled—but, on the other hand, there was no new development.

The weekend passed and I kept searching diligently for employment on the Internet. Nothing satisfactory turned up.

The following Monday in mid-afternoon I received a telephone call. A strange, but pleasant male voice courteously informed me that it was about the position for which I had applied eleven days before. The call was from the person himself who needed an employee.

He asked me to meet with him for an interview on the following day.

Really?

Really!!

The position was offered to me.

It is a very good position in a particularly beautiful location.

I now work with kind, caring, decent people.

> **"O Lord, the hope of Israel . . . thou art my praise."**[3]

16

Let go the past

"Remember ye not the former things, neither consider the things of old. Behold, I will do a new thing; now it shall spring forth; shall ye not know."

—Isaiah 43: 18-19 (KJV)

On the day that I decided to forgive, let go and move on the Prayer Team had e-mailed me: **"By your act you are now in a position to receive more blessings than you could ever believe, simply because you chose to do His will and serve Jesus. Be blessed!"**

On April 20 I followed up by asking the prayer team to pray with me for right employment.

In their reply the team said: **"We join with you in giving God praise for the many opportunities He has for each of us, and we ask that He opens a**

door which no one can close, showing you an employment opportunity that will be of benefit to you. We pray also that His timing is perfect so that you clearly see His hand in this matter, in Jesus Name."

On April 23 in mid-afternoon I received the phone call that set up the interview for the following day April 24.

Epilogue

God is.

I know that.

He truly is, indeed, A Very Present Help in time of trouble.

= The end=

Endnotes

Introduction
Divine Appointments and Divine Connections

1. The Higher Pantheism 1809 Alfred Lord Tennyson
2. 1 Peter 5:10 King James Version
3. 1 Peter 4:12 King James Version
4. J.C. Phillpott: Daily Portions January 13, 2013
5. Zechariah 13:9 King James Version
6. 1 Peter 5:10 King James Version
7. Psalm 119:71
8. Matthew 17:20 King James Version
9. 1 Kings 19: 12
10. Isaiah 45:5 King James Version
11. Isaiah 46: 9 & 10
12. Daniel 3.
13. Deuteronomy 31: 6
14. Isaiah 43: 2 New Living Translation 2007
15. Isaiah 42.16 King James Version
17. Psalm 6 King James Version
18. Romans 8 v 28 NIV 1984
19. Psalm 27:14 King James Version
20. Psalm 37:7 King James Version

21. Psalm 37:34 King James Version
22. Psalm 130: 5 King James Version
23. Psalm 85: 8 King James Version

Chapter 3

1. Genesis 3:1 King James Version
2. "Everything Crash!" The first big hit by the Jamaican Rock Steady Group known as *The Ethiopians* recorded in 1968.
3. Ephesians 6:12 King James Version
4. Job 8:10
5. Psalm 31:13 King James Version
6. Psalm 55:12 King James Version
7. 2nd Samuel 24:14 King James Version
8. Psalm 103:14 King James Version
9. Luke 15 11-32 King James Version
10. St. Matthew 7 v: 3 King James Version
11. J. C. Phillpot Daily Portions October 7, 2012
12. Psalm 3 v: 1 & 2
13. Psalm 102 v: 4

Chapter 4

1. Hebrews 10: 35-36 NIV
2. 1 Samuel 30: 6 King James Version
3. Jeff Doles: How to Encourage Yourself in the Lord.

Chapter 5

1. Isaiah 54 v: 17 King James Version

Chapter 6

1. St. Matthew 6 v. 31 King James Version
2. Psalm 124 v1-3
3. St. Matthew 5 v 42 King James Version

Chapter 7

1. Alexander Pope—1688-1744. Encyclopedia of World Biography states that Pope is regarded as one of the finest English poets.

Chapter 8

1. William Shakespeare

Chapter 9

1. James 5 v16 King James Version

Chapter 10

1. Job 30:16 King James Version

Chapter 11

1. Psalm 23 v: 4 King James Version
3. Agape Love—selfless, sacrificial and unconditional love—About.com Christianity
4. The Valley of Achor—Hosea 2:15

Chapter 12

1. Ruth 1 v: 16 King James Version

Chapter 13

1. Job 14:14 King James Version
2. Job 14:14 King James Version

Chapter 14

1. Mark Ch.11: 25 King James Version
2. Psalm 37.1, King James Version
3. 1 Corinthians 10:13 New International Version
4. Psalm 55:22 (King James Bible, Cambridge Edition.
5. Psalm 19:10, King James Version.
6. Steve Maraboli, Life, the Truth and Being Free
7. Mary-Alice and Richard Jafolla, The Lazarus Blueprint, *ancient secrets for healing and inner peace.* Unity Books.
8. Eckhart Tulle, **A New Earth** Awakening to Your Life's Purpose.
9. Alfred Lord Tennyson (1809-1892)
10. Heb. 13: 6 King James Version

11. Psalm 126 verses 1& 2 King James Version
12. Deuteronomy 31:8 King James Version

Chapter 15

1. Isaiah 46.10
2. Romans 8: 28
3. Jeremiah 17: 13,14 (KJV)

About the Author

Barbara Jones Nelson was born in Jamaica and educated at the University of the West Indies, Mona, Jamaica and Exeter University, Devon, England.

She taught for some time at the secondary level in Jamaica after graduating from University. Then she went into journalism where she was a newspaper reporter, feature writer, researcher and proofreader and for many years a Book Reviewer for *The Gleaner* newspaper.

Barbara co-authored with Ruby King and Pansy Robinson the Social Studies Book "***Our People, Our Heritage, Our Life***" for Jamaican schools.

Barbara now lives in the United States.